Greenland and Grenada

BY KIM THOMPSON

A Little Honey Book

Tips for Teachers and Caregivers

This book supports early readers as they decode words to learn facts and gain knowledge about the world.

Before reading, make sure students understand the sound-spelling correspondences shown below as well as the high-frequency words shown on the next page. Introduce the vocabulary words.

During reading, provide feedback and encouragement as students sound out decodable words by blending individual sounds.

After reading, talk about and write about the topic. Share the information on page 16 to help students learn more.

Letters and Sounds

New:

consonant blends with *r*, including *br, cr, dr, fr, gr, pr, scr, str,* and *tr*

Review:

all consonant sounds and standard spellings; *short a* spelled *a, short e* spelled *e, short i* spelled *i, short o* spelled *o, short u* spelled *u*

Decodable Words

an, and, big, brims, brisk, crab, cram, crests, crusts, drafts, dress, drift, fox, frigid, frog, frost, grand, grass, has, hats, hot, in, is, jump, land, not, on, ox, plants, press, sand, scrub, snug, strands, strut, tracks, tramp, trap, trek, trip, trunks, winds

High-Frequency Words

New: cold, come, green, little, one, see, together, warm

Review: a, are, by, could, do, live, make, of, or, people, the, there, they, to, white, with, you

Vocabulary Words

fish

Greenland

Grenada

houses

islands

tree

Come on a trip.

Trek to **Greenland**.
Tramp to **Grenada**.

They are **islands**.

One is big, and one is little.

Greenland is frigid.

Brisk winds make cold drafts.

Grenada is hot.

Warm winds drift by.

Greenland has
white crests.

Frost crusts the land.

Grenada has green crests.

There are strands of sand.

Greenland plants are scrub and grass.

You could see an ox or the tracks of a fox.

Grenada has grand **tree** trunks.

You could see a frog jump or a crab strut.

Houses do not cram on Greenland.

People trap **fish** to live.

Houses on Grenada press together.

People trap fish to live.

People on Greenland dress in snug hats.

People on Grenada dress in hats with brims.

Build Background Knowledge

Three times as large as the state of Texas, icy Greenland is the world's largest island. It has tundra, glaciers, and a massive ice sheet. Summer temperatures rise to an average of 42 degrees Fahrenheit (5.5 degrees Celsius). Grenada is a tropical island just 21 miles (34 kilometers) long. It lies in the Caribbean Sea, a basin of the Atlantic Ocean. The average temperature is 82 degrees Fahrenheit (28 degrees Celsius). Grenada has sandy beaches and forest-covered mountains.

GREENLAND AND GRENADA

Written by: Kim Thompson
Designed by: Rhea Magaro
Series Development: James Earley
Educational Consultant: Marie Lemke, M.Ed.

Photographs: All images from Shutterstock

Crabtree Publishing

crabtreebooks.com 800-387-7650

Printed in China/012024/FE20231222

Published in Canada
Crabtree Publishing
616 Welland Ave.
St. Catharines, Ontario
L2M 5V6

Published in the United States
Crabtree Publishing
347 Fifth Ave
Suite 1402-145
New York, NY 10016

Library and Archives Canada Cataloguing in Publication
Available at Library and Archives Canada

Library of Congress Cataloging-in-Publication Data
Available at the Library of Congress

Hardcover: 978-1-0398-4439-1
Paperback: 978-1-0398-4520-6
Ebook (pdf): 978-1-0398-4597-8
Epub: 978-1-0398-4667-8
Read-Along: 978-1-0398-4737-8
Audio: 978-1-0398-4807-8